JELLYFISH

A Buddy Book by
Deborah Coldiron

ABDO
Publishing Company

UNDERWATER WORLD

VISIT US AT
www.abdopublishing.com

Published by ABDO Publishing Company, 8000 West 78th Street, Edina, Minnesota 55439.

Printed in the United States.

Coordinating Series Editor: Sarah Tieck
Contributing Editor: Michael P. Goecke
Graphic Design: Deborah Coldiron
Cover Photograph: Minden Pictures: Mark Spencer/Auscape
Interior Photographs/Illustrations: Art Explosion (page 23); Animals Animals/Earth Scenes: E.R. Degginger (page 20), Keith Gillett (page 30); Minden Pictures: Mark Spencer/Auscape (page 7), Dr. David Wachenfeld/Auscape (page 28), National Oceanic and Atmospheric Administration (page 27); Norbert Wu (pages 13, 15, 17, 25, 29); Photodisc (page 25); Photos.com (pages 5, 9, 20, 21); Wikipedia Commons: Stan Shebs (pages 19, 27)

Library of Congress Cataloging-in-Publication Data

Coldiron, Deborah
     Jellyfish / Deborah Coldiron.
        p. cm. — (Underwater world)
     Includes index.
     ISBN 978-1-59928-810-9
      1. Jellyfishes—Juvenile literature. I. Title.

     QL377.S4C65 2007
     593.5'3—dc22

                                                              2007016264

Table Of Contents

The World Of Jellyfish

Every living creature needs water. Some animals not only need water, they live in it, too.

Scientists have found more than 250,000 kinds of plants and animals living underwater. And, they believe there could be one million more! The jellyfish is one animal that makes its home in this underwater world.

Seventy percent of Earth's surface is covered in water.

Jellyfish are **fragile** but powerful predators of the sea. The smallest are less than one inch (3 cm) wide. The largest jellyfish can grow to eight feet (2 m) across and more than 100 feet (30 m) long.

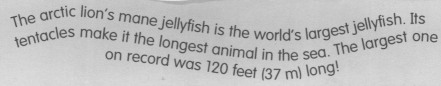

The arctic lion's mane jellyfish is the world's largest jellyfish. Its tentacles make it the longest animal in the sea. The largest one on record was 120 feet (37 m) long!

Arctic Lion's Mane Jellyfish

There are around 200 **species** of jellyfish in our underwater world. Jellyfish are found in oceans throughout the world. Some jellyfish-like creatures live in freshwater. But all true jellyfish live in salt water.

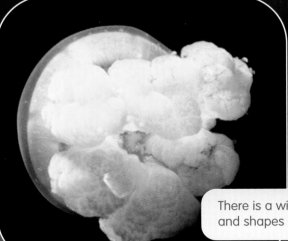

There is a wide variety of colors and shapes among jellyfish.

Ready For A Close-Up?

Jellyfish are **fragile** creatures. They have no bones, ears, eyes, or brains! Despite this, they are still very successful, feared predators.

FAST FACTS

Some jellyfish have light sensors. These sense sunlight coming through the water's surface. They help jellyfish determine which direction is up.

The Body Of A Jellyfish

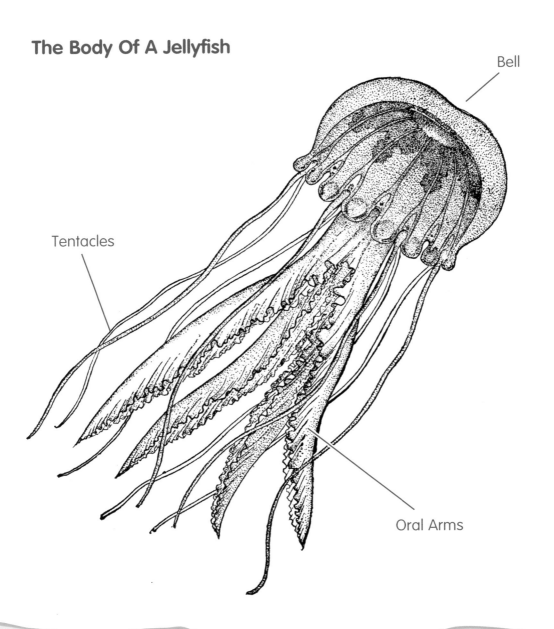

Bell

Tentacles

Oral Arms

A jellyfish body looks like a bell or an upside-down bowl. Its mouth is at the center of the bell's underside.

Some jellyfish may have four to eight frilly oral arms. These surround their mouths. Some also have stinging **tentacles**, which hang down from their bells.

Bell

Mouth

Tentacles

Amphipod

Oral Arms

Small crustaceans known as amphipods take shelter in the bells of some jellyfish.

Jellyfish swim by expanding and contracting their bell-shaped bodies. This looks much like an umbrella opening and closing.

When a jellyfish contracts its body, the water inside it is forced out. This moves the jellyfish forward. The process is a simple form of jet **propulsion**.

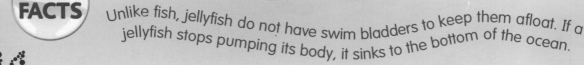

FAST FACTS Unlike fish, jellyfish do not have swim bladders to keep them afloat. If a jellyfish stops pumping its body, it sinks to the bottom of the ocean.

A jellyfish propels itself through water by opening and closing its bell.

A Growing Jellyfish

Most jellyfish go through several stages before becoming adults. A jellyfish begins life in an egg. The egg develops into a tiny planula. Then, the planula changes into a tubelike creature called a polyp.

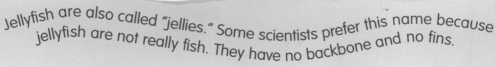

Jellyfish Polyps

A polyp usually attaches itself to the seafloor. Several jellyfish may form from a single polyp. Tiny pieces of the polyp detach and begin to float freely. These pieces, or medusas, are in the last stage before adulthood.

FAST FACTS

When a medusa detaches from a polyp, scientists call it "budding."

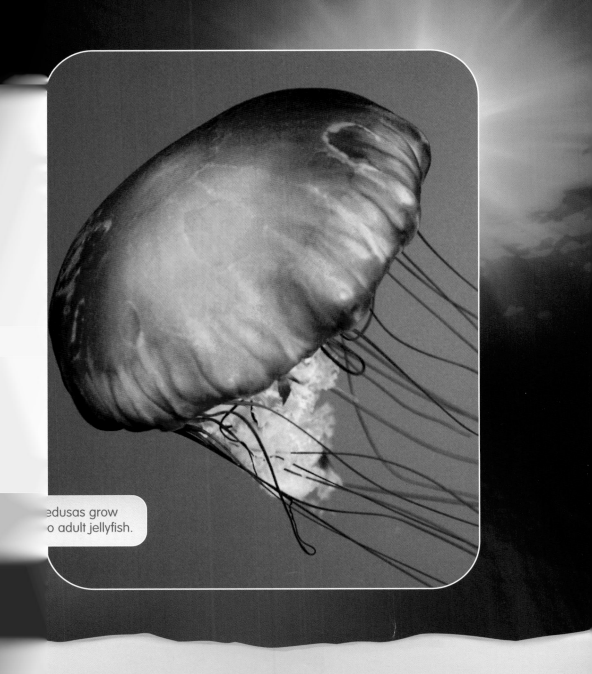

...edusas grow
...o adult jellyfish.

Family Fun

   Jellyfish belong to a group of animals called cnidarians (neye-DAYR-ee-uhns). There are about 9,000 **species** of cnidarians. Other cnidarians include sea anemones, sea fans, corals, and freshwater hydras.

Hydras are small freshwater creatures with several stinging tentacles.

Sea fans are a type of coral colony. The colonies form complex fan shapes.

Corals live together in colonies. Individual corals are called polyps.

Sea anemones look a lot like underwater flowering plants. Their flowing tentacles sting prey such as small fish.

A Big Neighborhood

Jellyfish are found in many areas of our oceans. So, a list of all their neighbors would be quite long!

One of the jellyfish's most common neighbors is zooplankton. Zooplankton are tiny animals that float along in the ocean's **currents**.

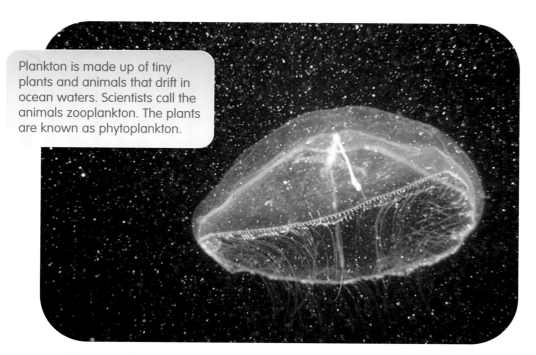

Plankton is made up of tiny plants and animals that drift in ocean waters. Scientists call the animals zooplankton. The plants are known as phytoplankton.

Zooplankton includes many small **invertebrates** and young animals in their larval stages. Jellyfish feed on these small animals. So do many larger ocean animals, such as large baleen whales.

Waiting For Dinner

Jellyfish are **carnivores**. Most jellyfish feed on tiny creatures that drift into contact with their stinging **tentacles**. Sometimes they will even eat small fish.

Jellyfish tentacles are well equipped for hunting food. They contain stinging cells that explode when they come into contact with prey. Then, the stinging cells shoot tiny threads of **toxins** into the animal. This **paralyzes** the prey.

FAST FACTS

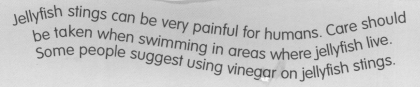

Jellyfish stings can be very painful for humans. Care should be taken when swimming in areas where jellyfish live. Some people suggest using vinegar on jellyfish stings.

Some jellyfish have just a few tentacles. Others may have hundreds.

Danger Zone

For jellyfish, the oceans are dangerous. Many animals eat jellyfish. These include ocean sunfish, blue rockfish, and sea turtles. Some large sea snails and birds have also been known to feast on jellyfish.

FAST FACTS

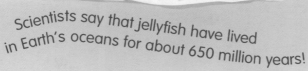

Scientists say that jellyfish have lived in Earth's oceans for about 650 million years!

Sea Snail

Blue Rockfish

Ocean Sunfish

Sea Turtle

27

Fascinating Facts

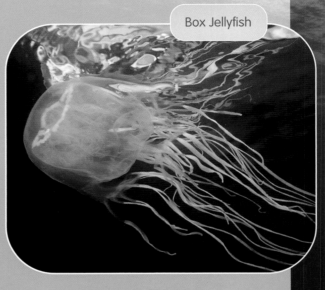

Box Jellyfish

Box jellyfish are among the most deadly creatures in the ocean! If a human is stung by one of these jellyfish, he or she may die within minutes. These jellyfish are sometimes called sea wasps. They live off the coasts of Australia, the Philippines, and other **tropical** locations.

The Portuguese man-of-war looks a lot like a jellyfish. But, these **gelatinous** masses are actually made up of hundreds of tiny animals. These animals work together in a **colony**. Because they sting like jellyfish, care must be taken even when they wash up dead on the beach.

Portuguese Man-Of-War

Learn And Explore

Scientists at James Cook University in Queensland, Australia, have discovered jellyfish that sleep!

Using a special glue, the researchers fitted box jellyfish with tiny trackers. They found one **species** was active from about 6 AM until 3 PM. After 3 PM, the jellyfish rest on the ocean floor until morning. The scientists think sleep helps them keep up with their fast-growing bodies.

Box Jellyfish

IMPORTANT WORDS

carnivore meat-eater.

colony a group of animals of one kind living together.

current the flow and movement of a large body of water.

fragile easily broken, damaged, or destroyed.

gelatinous jellylike.

invertebrate an animal with no backbone.

paralyze to make unable to move.

propulsion something that drives forward or adds speed to an object.

species living things that are very much alike.

tentacle a long, slender body part that grows around the mouth or head of some animals.

toxin a substance that is harmful.

tropical an area on Earth where temperatures are warm.

WEB SITES

To learn more about the jellyfish, visit ABDO Publishing Company on the World Wide Web. Web sites about jellyfish are featured on our Book Links page. These links are routinely monitored and updated to provide the most current information available.

www.abdopublishing.com

INDEX